HowExpert

CW01455959

Horse C_____ ___

How to Take Care of a
Horse for Beginners

HowExpert with
Karin Bauer

**For more tips related to this topic,
visit HowExpert.com/horse.**

Recommended Resources

- HowExpert.com – Quick 'How To' Guides on All Topics from A to Z by Everyday Experts.
- HowExpert.com/free – Free HowExpert Email Newsletter.
- HowExpert.com/books – HowExpert Books
- HowExpert.com/courses – HowExpert Courses
- HowExpert.com/clothing – HowExpert Clothing
- HowExpert.com/membership – HowExpert Membership Site
- HowExpert.com/affiliates – HowExpert Affiliate Program
- HowExpert.com/writers – Write About Your #1 Passion/Knowledge/Expertise & Become a HowExpert Author.
- HowExpert.com/resources – Additional HowExpert Recommended Resources
- YouTube.com/HowExpert – Subscribe to HowExpert YouTube.
- Instagram.com/HowExpert – Follow HowExpert on Instagram.
- Facebook.com/HowExpert – Follow HowExpert on Facebook.

Table of Contents

Chapter 1: Bringing Your Equine Companion Home

Introducing Your Horse to His New Home

I can write this article based on my own experience. When I was 13 years old, my parents bought me a pinto gelding named Dexter. Dexter's previous owners kept him outside, then when we bought him and brought him to the stable, we wondered how Dexter (and we) would handle the transition. We knew this was something that would take time and work.

Your new equine companion has arrived. He is nervous and is looking around. He does not know where he is at or what is going to happen to him. You must get him adjusted. What do you do?

One important piece of information is that you speak with the former owner on how much hay, grain (and what type) and pasture time the horse gets. Sudden changes in a horse's food and turn out/stall time can cause serious complications.

I will explain an experience based on owning Dexter. Because Dexter was kept outside, and we moved him to a box stall, the transition took a toll on him. Dexter was quite ill. Perhaps it was the stress of being in a new environment or it was the new food. Before buying Dexter, he was never in a box stall. After time, tender loving care and veterinary care, Dexter recovered, and was more energetic than ever. When it was safe to ride him again, Dexter was happy and playful, and bucked me off! I did not get hurt but I was happy Dexter recovered and was in good spirits.

A transition as described above can cause a horse to fall ill. When transitioning a completely outdoor horse to a box stall, it must be done gradually. Although Dexter took to the box stall quite well quickly, it does not mean every horse will.

A Place to Call Home

You cannot read a horse's mind, so you never know if he wants to move or not. If the horse could talk to you, possibly he would say "I don't want to move! I like it here. I have many friends. I don't want to leave them." Many people, especially children who relocate to a new neighborhood and school, can feel that way. Just like how the children miss their friends from their old neighborhood, the horse feels the same way when he is moved to a new farm.

However, as I explained earlier about Dexter, sometimes a relocated horse becomes happier in their new home. You never know what the result will be until you actually go through with it. Horses are individuals just like humans. Sometimes when humans relocate, they become happier in their new homes, while others want to move back to their old home.

Although Dexter adjusted to his new home rather quick, some horses can get homesick and take a long time to adjust to their new home.

While in many cases, humans relocate voluntarily. The horse probably did not make the choice to relocate. Horses are usually more resistant to change than humans are. That is why this event is more stressful for him that it is for you. You understand what is going on. He does not.

If you buy a horse that went through some tormenting and mistreatment, then you are doing a good thing by relocating him. Still, the horse does not know what he will go through. He will not know whether or not he will get good treatment in his new home. So, it is up to you to show the horse that you are going to give him a good, loving home.

Dexter went through some mistreatment by his previous owners. My parents and I worked on (and it took some work) showing him that not all humans are "evil". Dexter became a friendly, trusting horse after a long time of tender loving care.

Horses do not know the "do not judge all on the act of one" story. A mistreated horse can view all humans as a threat.

Stop Stressing Me Out!

Just like humans, stress takes a toll on a horse's mental and physical health. The horse does not know how to relieve his own anxiety, so you have to do it for him.

Horses help humans relieve stress. Riding and looking after horses can help ease stress on humans, but what about the other way around? You can give your horse a stress relief counseling session. Besides from the horse not being able to talk to you, you can counsel your horse like another human. No, horses cannot practice yoga or meditation. Although it would be nice if they could!

Last but not least, you must make sure your new horse is up to date on all vaccinations and tested negative on the Coggins test. Horses are prone to infectious diseases while under stress.

Who Are You and What Are You Doing Here?

The long-time resident horses of your farm may not accept your new arrival right away. This can be compared to a new student in school who is often picked on by the current students.

I was concerned about Dexter becoming aggressive towards other horses because of his prior experiences. To some extent, Dexter was a bully victim. So was I when I was a child in school. Well, I can say Dexter and I had something in common.

I kept Dexter in a pasture separate from the long-time resident horses, however, not solitary confinement.

Horses, by nature, are herd animals. Dexter was kept in an adjacent pasture, so if in the event he is bullied by the other horses, Dexter will be able to get away without being pursued by the bully horses.

What I explained above is a recommended method when bringing your new horse home. Until you are sure your new horse is not aggressive towards other horses, you can slowly adjust him being around the long-time resident horses.

Sometimes when we meet new people, we can become good friends almost right away. I know I had my experiences during childhood, where it was like we became best friends instantly. But horses – less so. New horses need time to learn to get along with each other. You may see them flattening their ears at each other at first, but over time they can learn to get along.

Dexter became friends with some horses, but then he had his enemies, too.

While I did not fight back bullies, Dexter was different. Dexter got attached to a buckskin mare and they became a pair. I saw Dexter kick with both hind legs at other horses when they got too close to the mare. Dexter also had some kick marks on his legs. I saw Dexter challenge larger horses. Dexter was 15.1 hands high, and he challenged a horse that was almost 17 hands! That would be like someone fighting someone almost a foot taller. However, Dexter went that extra mile to protect his girlfriend.

As I explained earlier, your new horse will not get along with the other horses overnight. Adjusting him to his new companions may take time. Who knows, your new horse may find a "main squeeze"!

Remember the two main items – time and patience.

If your new horse is a bully victim, keep him in his own field away from the other horses, but still with other horses in sight. The bully victim horse must not think he is being punished, not to mention he will have no idea what he is punished for.

As with people, relocation for a horse causes stress, and he will not always fit in with the other horses right away. With the two main items mentioned earlier, time and patience, it will all work out. You should see improvement over time.

Chapter 2: Feeding

Introducing a New Food

Some people are resistant when it comes to eating habits or trying new foods. Horses are the same way.

Did you ever have an adverse reaction to foods you have never eaten before? Such as when you travel to a foreign country and you eat the local cuisine, you did not feel too well? This is because your body is not used to the food. The same thing can happen to when your horse is in his new home and eats the stable's "local cuisine".

If you provide a different type of food that was different than what the horse was fed before, keep a bag or two of his current food and feed him that first.

The concept is the same when you change your dog's or cat's brand of food. The transition is slow and gradual to prevent digestive issues.

If your horse was never fed grain before, feed him very small amounts starting once a day. If you find his body handles the grain, then gradually increase the servings to two or three times a day.

Keep an eye on him as he eats his new food. If a horse develops an allergic reaction, it can take a while before the symptoms occur. Wait several days, or even longer, before getting him completely on the new food.

Proper Feeding

Provide plenty of roughage for your horse. A horse's body is meant for roughage, not grain mixed with molasses (the molasses provides the sugar to give the horse energy). Horses did not eat grain when they were wild. Good quality hay and pasture grass is good for all horses, whether the horses are for equestrian events or pleasure rides. Grain is a good supplement when hay or grass is not sufficient. Grain also provides extra nutrients and protein for sport or working horses.

Grain should be fed in small amounts and in intervals, such as one scoop three times a day. Too much gain fed at once can cause stomach issues, even colic.

Never give a horse grain right before or after immediately after exercise. Wait at least an hour, or closer to three hours is the exercise is strenuous.

If you ever exercised right after eating, you get a stomach cramp and want to lie down. A horse cannot do this. A horse will want to lie down when he has an upset stomach.

However, a difference occurs when it comes to breathing. You may wonder what a full stomach has to be with breathing. When a human has a full stomach, it does not impact breathing. However, when a horse's stomach is full, it gives the lungs less room to work. This is the reason behind not exercising a horse right after he eats grain. The grain fills the horse's stomach more than grass or hay does.

A horse can breathe only through his nostrils. When the lungs do not have the room to work due to an overfilled stomach, it causes breathing difficulty. A horse cannot use his mouth as a breathing "backup", that is, they cannot pant like a dog.

Where's my Treat?

We know horses love treats. The old-fashioned treated are sugar cubes, carrots, and apples. I gave Dexter these treats. Back then I knew nothing about baked treats or did not know if they even existed. While these may have been given to horses for years, sometimes these can cause problems. Horses love the taste of sweets like humans do, however, sugar is a health hazard for horses as it is for humans.

Carrots have natural sugar, which is why horses love them. Carrots can be given to horses as a treat, if they are washed first (due to increased use of pesticides) and in moderation. Too many treats of any times can cause a severe stomach discomfort or even colic. We know your horse's sad eyes may be hard to resist, but still do not feed him too many carrots.

I brought Dexter carrots every time I went to the stable. Dexter knew it, too. When I opened the stable door, I saw Dexter look at me with his ears forward. He knew what I had!

Apples also have natural sugar. The problem with apples is that the seeds contain a small amount of a toxic chemical. People used to give their horses whole apples and then the toxins in the seeds caused a sickness. People thought the horse had an allergic reaction to apples (however, some horses really do) but it was the seeds causing the illness. Yes, even tiny apple seeds can get a large animal like a horse sick. Give your horse sliced apples and throw the core away.

You can find baked treats for horses (I did not know about these when I had Dexter) at your local feed store or online marketplaces like Amazon. These are like biscuits or cookies but made for horses. They are made with apples, carrots, oats, molasses, etc. and do not contain chemicals or animal products such as milk or eggs.

Proper feeding techniques, including introducing a new food, should all be followed carefully to avoid the stress of your horse getting sick. If you ever moved to a foreign country, getting used to that country's food may take time. Same with the new food your horse is fed in his new home.

Chapter 3: Housing

Introducing an Outdoor Horse to a Stall

Dexter was kept outside. Moving him to a box stall was a life-changing event for him. However, over time, he learned to love the stall. In fact, sometimes it was hard to get Dexter out of the stall!

Dexter was an outdoor horse, so he had to fight for his food. He saw the stall as his own world and a place to be safe and secure rom other horses and have his own food. The stall became his sanctuary.

People view their homes as their sanctuaries. Horses feel the same way about their stalls.

If your horse was kept mostly outdoors and you are introducing him to a box stall, introduction must be slow and pleasant. The idea is to get the horse to associate the stall with food and safety - not a prison. You do not want him to go "stir crazy".

Have a large stall available, with plenty of bedding and the horse's current food (not the new food you are transitioning him to). The horse wants some "memories" of his former home. The food he is used to will help. When he smells it, he will want to eat it, whether he is hungry.

Horses are the type of animals will always eat regardless of how full they are. Rarely will a horse refuse food. He would have to be quite ill to refuse food.

The horse may throw a fit and pace around in the stall and kick. You will want a large stall to give him plenty of room to move around so he does not feel so confined. Stay nearby or have someone else stay near to check on the horse. It will take the time for the horse to learn he is not being held prisoner or not being punished.

Never leave a nervous or frightened horse in a stall unattended. Do not attempt to remove the horse from the stall while he is panicking. Keep talking to him in a soft tone of voice. Do not yell or crack a whip. This will scare him more.

When he calms down, you can put him back out to the field. You can gradually increase his stall time each day and feed him a little grain and treats when he is calm in his stall. When the horse learns, he will have his own food supply in his stall, he will have good thoughts about the stall. Pasture horses fight for their food, so your horse may still have that instinct to fight when he has food and other horses are nearby. This was especially true with Dexter. However, you still do not want to keep him in the stall for long periods of time.

One recommendation is to have the grain ready in his feed bin when bringing the horse in from the pasture. That way he will go right in the stall knowing his food is already there. This will prevent bad thoughts about the stall.

The Great Outdoors

By nature, horses are outdoor animals. When they were wild, they were not in stalls. When severe weather hit, wild horses would seek shelter under trees to for protection from rain and the hot sun or stand in a gully to be shielded from wind.

Most domestic horses, especially ones kept in barns, do not have these survival skills that their wild ancestors had. When "indoor" horses are out in the pasture and a storm brews, the horses will want back in the barn immediately.

Thunder and lightning can be frightening to horses (as well as to people).

Imagine you are outside walking a thunderstorms brews. You start to panic and then seek shelter immediately. Horses feel the same way.

If you insist on keeping your horse outdoors because you cannot adjust him to a stall, then have a run-in shelter available in the pasture. These are like stalls except that the horse can enter and leave when he wants. He will have a safe place from severe weather such as thunderstorms.

Run-in shelters also provide shade from the hot summer sun. A horses' skin and coat can get sunburn, especially on the tips of their noses or around the eyes, where the skin is bare. Excessive sunlight also fades a dark horse's coat.

Just like when you are at the beach, you like to lie under the beach umbrella. Sunburns hurts! Horses can also feel pain from sunburn.

Horses and humans enjoy being outdoors. The great outdoors can an incredible experience when we know how to play it safe – for us and the horses.

Natural Shelter

As explained earlier, wild horses used trees as protection from rain and the hot sun. Trees also make good shady spots, as well as shelter from the rain, which is more natural for the horse. If there are no shade trees in the pasture and you would like to add some, consider some safe, fast-growing trees such as a Freeman Maple, Sweetgum or Weeping Willow. These are the types of trees that when they drop their leaves in the autumn, the horse is not harmed by eating the leaves, however, the horse may find the leaves foul-tasting and will not eat them.

Avoid Red Maples because the leaves and bark are toxic to horses. A White Pine is also a safe shade tree but those should be avoided in you live in an area with high air pollution.

Do not plant fruit trees out in the pasture. Horses will gorge on the fruit and can become sick. Fruit trees also attract unwanted visitors such as raccoons, deer, foxes, excessive bird flocks, and even bears, depending on where you live. Horses may be less than enthusiastic about sharing their pasture with those animals. Worse of all, (depending on where you live) fruit trees can attract bears. Bears near a horse farm can cause severe chaos.

Certain trees like those described in this chapter may look pretty in the pasture, but safety comes before beauty. Nobody wants a horse harmed from trees that pose a threat to horses.

Chapter 4: When to Call a Vet

Fortunately, Dexter never had any medical emergencies. The only time we needed a vet was when shortly after he was moved to the stable, when he got sick (which I explained in the first chapter). We thought it was the change of environment, from being kept outside and moved to a stable. That just happened that one time, and Dexter never had an illness since.

Equine emergencies are unavoidable. No matter how much you keep your horse in good health, a problem will arise sooner or later. Owning a horse can be no different than having a child. Health issues come up in horses just like they do in children.

Finding Abnormal Signs

The most important signs to know are your horse's vital signs, such as pulse, respiration, and temperature. We know what is normal for people, and horse owners must know what is normal for horses.

Grooming your horse is a good way to find cuts, scrapes and lumps that are not easily visible. Grooming helps find other issues such as sensitive spots caused by a recent injury.

Sometimes a relaxed horse will stand with his head level and lower lip hanging. The lower lip hanging is not always a sign of illness. When you enter your horse's stall, he should react, at least by looking at you with his ears forward. If the horse does not react to you coming into his stall, and remains standing with his lip hanging, then that may be an abnormal sign.

Signs Telling You to Call a Vet Immediately

These signs may not seem so serious, but they are. In fact, some can be life-threatening.

Injuries with uncontrollable bleeding.

Obvious fractures.

Injury accompanies by swelling.

Cut that require stitches.

Labored breathing when the horse was not exercised.

Choking. The worse kind if when the horse has his neck stretched and discharge from nostrils.

Seizures.

Watery diarrhea.

Eye Injury.

Signs of Colic

When a horse has a blockage in his intestine, colic can occur. Horses do not vomit. Because of this, the horse is in excruciating pain when the stomach contents cannot be excreted through the mouth.

Colic is the twisting of the gut caused by a blockage or by excessive gas. The main cause is overeating or eating too fast. Moldy foods or a food intolerance, especially grains, can also cause colic. Severe constipation occurs, and the horse is unable to defecate. The horse's belly may bloat from gas causing pain and discomfort. The horse will make every attempt to relieve the pain but will not have success.

The horse cannot talk to you and tell you he has a blockage in his gut. That is why you need to know the signs.

These are the most common symptoms of colic:

- Anxiety or depression
- Excessive pawing
- Excessive rolling
- Looking and biting at his flanks
- Attempting to kick his belly with hind leg
- Lack of appetite
- Lying down longer than normal

When a horse has colic, there is no way to avoid calling the vet. Nor is there any excuse. Call the vet immediately.

Veterinary treatment involves use of analgesics to control the pain. The impaction can be softened by laxatives or mineral oil. When the pain is under control and the horse can get up on his feet, you can walk him around to help loosen the impaction. Walking helps humans relieve constipation. The concept is the same with horses.

Hold off on feeding, but provide plenty of water, until the impaction has been released through defecation.

Providing plenty of fresh drinking water can help prevent colic. Other ways to prevent colic is to watch grain intake and avoid excessive confinement in the stall.

Horses kept in the stall too long get bored and develop a bad habit called cribbing. This is when the horse latches his upper jaw to the wood of the stall, opens his mouth, and sucks in large amount of air. You will hear a loud sound, remotely sounding like a gasp of air. This is different than wood chewing. Cribbing is another cause of colic.

Stall Confinement and Colic

Giving your horse ample pasture time and less confinement in the stall will reduce the chances of developing cribbing and other complications caused by inactivity. This will result in reducing the risk of colic.

This can be compared to a person who works an office job and spends long hours sitting at a desk. Those people develop health problems, such as blood clots and even heart disease, from the lack of activity. Those people who sit at their desk long hours may not have a choice (although they could have the choice of taking the day off from work). The concept is the same with horses. The horse cannot leave his stall by choice. Therefore, it is up to you to give him time out of the stall and run around in the field.

Sedentary lifestyles are a hazard to horses as well as to people. Horses, by nature, are active animals. In the wild, they kept roaming and roaming. Allow horses to keep their natural instinct of "wild and free" by giving ample pasture time. Physical activity improves a horse's lifestyle and well-being, as it does for humans.

Chapter 5: Skin, Coat and Hoof Care.

Horse owners often do not think much of the horse's skin in terms of good health. The horse's coat covers his skin; therefore, people concentrate on the coat.

The horse's skin is not just for providing a base for his coat. A horse's skin is also an organ. The skin provides a defense against injury and infection. The skin also provides a cooling system by sweating. Horses, besides humans, are one of the very few animals that sweat. The horse's skin also stores water and fats (this is not compared to a camel's hump).

A horse's healthy skin leads to a healthy coat. You want your horse's coat to be smooth and shiny. Daily grooming lets you find any coat or skin issues that you cannot easily see.

Itchy and Scratchy

A horse that has been exercised has heavy sweat under the saddle and can make him itch. When you remove the saddle, and let the horse out in the field, the first thing he will do is roll to relieve the back itch. This is a form of self-grooming. Most people do not bother bathing the horse after exercise because the horse will roll on the ground once he is put out in the field. However, it is still a good idea to bathe the horse to remove the sweat. Just hosing him with water will do; no need to use soap. Sweat drying on his coat can lead to skin and coat issues. If you would rather not bathe the horse, such as if the weather is not warm enough, a good grooming will help remove the sweat.

When using a shampoo, use one specifically for horses. Shampooing is not always necessary and should not be done every day. Excessive shampooing removes the natural oils on the horse's coat. The horse needs those oils to keep his coat healthy and shiny.

You may think "but people wash their hair every day." Human shampoos have no comparison to horse shampoos. People, especially women, can wash their hair every day to remove styling products such as hair spray and gels. Human shampoos are meant for daily cleansing. Horse shampoos are not.

Good grooming tools and coat and skin supplements will help relieve itching. Keeping back itch under control will help prevent the horse from rolling in the stall. Horses can end up in danger by rolling in the stall. Some issues are hoof problems from kicking the stall walls. Worse of all they can be trapped in the rolling position. The stall provides limited room to allow the horse to get back on his feet.

Do not tie the horse in his stall to prevent him from rolling. The itchy back will cause him distress which will then cause anxiety. He could injure himself and cause damage to the stall. In addition, if the rope is long enough for the horse to lie down, he could injure his neck and spine while trying to roll. Worse of all the horse become trapped in a bad position and may not be able to get up.

Imagine you had an itchy back and you are tied to a chair and unable to move to scratch your back. That would drive you crazy. The horse feels the same way if he is tied and unable to roll. Rolling is a horse's instinct to relieve back itch.

Depending on the horse's skin condition, grooming him could make him itch more. If this is the case, do not groom him, and give the horse an external skin supplement, such as an oil-based spray to relieve dry skin. Do not use human body lotions on horses.

Horses can consume canola oil. Canola oil (this is preferred over corn oil) helps the coat produce oils to moisturize the skin, and it makes his coat shiny. Mix a little canola oil with his grain so he will consume the oil.

Horses (along with many other herbivores) do not have gall bladders; therefore, they cannot digest fats as well as humans can. That is why oil is to be used in moderation. Excessive oil can cause digestive issues. If you would rather avoid the risk and not use oil, you can use rice bran, linseed and chia. These are high in omega-3's and are more digestible than oils.

Although horses and cattle are designed to eat grass, their digestive systems are not related in any way. A horse's digestive system is somewhat similar to a human's, and not to a cow's. Horses do not chew cuds like cattle. Like humans, horses have an appendix, however, a horse's appendix is needed for survival as a species, while humans can live without an appendix.

Hoof Care

The horse's hoof wall is a shield that covers the sensitive internal tissues. The hoof is made of a tough protein called keratin. Keratin is also found in a human's finger and toe nails and a bull's horns. Just like a human's fingernails, a horse's hoof can become dry and cracked and will need treatment.

Watch for diseases such as laminitis. This is often caused by excess sugars in the horse's diet. These cause the hoof to be abnormally shaped, such as "bell-shaped" or rippling in the hooves. Laminitis also thins the soles of the feet and causes sensitivity and pain.

Some horses' hooves have thin walls. The wall – not the sole- is thin and does not protect the inside which has the nerves. These horses' owners use synthetic shoes such as glue-on boots. Those types of shoes do not use nails, therefore, there is no risk of a nail hitting a sensitive spot.

Shoeing Your Horse

The horse's hoof wall is all bone. This is the part where horseshoes are nailed. The horse can only feel in the triangular part on the bottom called the frog (it is unknown how it got called the "frog"). The horseshoe nails are nowhere near that area.

The frog may shed about twice a year. This is normal. You may not always notice this because when your farrier is shoeing your horse, he may trim off the shedding skin. The frog is the only part of the hoof that has nerves. If the hoof is trimmed too low and the frog touches the ground, that will cause pain. This is because the horse is bearing his weight on the frog. To a person, that would feel like walking barefoot on a gravel road. Ouch!

Horses for show jumping often have silicone pads on their front feet. The front feet are the load-bearing feet when landing over the fence. The silicone pads act like cushions for their feet, sort of like those Dr. Scholl's shock absorbers for a human's athletic shoes.

Dexter had silicone pads on his front feet during his show jumping days. They helped protect his front hooves from damage.

Cleaning Your Horse's Feet

When a horse has a stone stuck on his hoof, it is often stuck on the frog. This can cause the horse discomfort. This would be like getting sand or a stone in your shoe. You can remove your shoe to remove the sand or stone, but the horse cannot remove it himself. Cleaning out the horse's hoof with a hoof pick and a brush can remove stones and dirt and make him comfortable.

The horse's hoofs should be picked before and after riding to remove any objects that got lodged in his foot.

Horses know the drill – they see the hoofpick and know when you are going to clean his feet. Dexter was good at this. When I came towards his feet with the hoofpick, he would lift his foot up and allow me to clean it.

Hoof Supplements

A hoof supplement, such as a hoof cream or oil, should be applied regularly to prevent the hoof from drying and cracking. Hoof drying and cracking if often caused by cold weather or in areas where the air is dry. Some hoof creams applied by hand are known to strengthen your fingernails! These supplements will keep your horse's feet strong and healthy.

Some supplements, either taken by mouth or applied directly to the foot, are for the soles of the horse's feet. These can help strengthen the sole and thicken the skin on the frog to protect his feet. These supplements also help reduce sensitivity on the soles on the horse's feet.

A horse's skin, coat and feet require the same care as for people. People want healthy skin, hair and nails. Horses want healthy skin, coat and hooves. Horses cannot treat their own skin, coat and hooves, so it is up to us to do it for them.

Chapter 6: Bad Habits

Cribbing – The Most Common

Just like humans, horses can have bad habits. They can pick up bad habits from the other horses, or these habits just come naturally. Another name for a horse's bad habit is called a vice.

When we walk into the stable, we hear the normal sounds of horses – eating they hay or giving a little nicker when their owner enters the barn. The most unpleasant sound is a horse cribbing.

Luckily, Dexter was not a cribber nor had any of the bad habits explained in this chapter. Some of his neighbor horses were, however, it is not a proven fact that a horse starts cribbing because a horse near him is a cribber. Nothing is proven about horses picking up bad habits from each other or horses imitating another's bad habits. Horses can "feed off" from each other in other ways, but not cause bad habits like cribbing.

Cribbing was briefly discussed in a previous chapter. Cribbing is one of the most prevalent bad habits. Cribbing, also known as "wind-sucking" is a hard habit to break. Cribbing is a cause of colic and other health issues, including dental problems. Cribbing also causes damage to the stall door.

Cribbing can be compared to a human smoking. They are both addictions. Once a horse starts cribbing, it takes work to get him to stop, just like how it takes work to get a human to stop smoking.

This bad habit (vice) of often controlled by a cribbing collar. The cribbing collar is viewed as a controversial device and not all people use it on their cribbing horses. The collar is placed on the upper part of the horse's neck with a metal piece around the throat. The horse can still eat and drink, but the metal piece on the collar prevents the horse from expanding his esophagus, thus allowing him to swallow less air.

The horses can still swallow air with the cribbing collar on, but just not as much. However, this is not a "cure" for cribbing. Colic or other disorders from cribbing can still eventually develop. In other words, the cribbing collar can slow down the developing of colic but not prevent it.

You can provide toys to the horse, such as the Horseman's Pride Jolly Ball, to relieve boredom. This may not completely deter cribbing, but it will keep the horse occupies to reduce cribbing. There is no known "cure" for cribbing.

Horses can use fence posts for cribbing. If you use a cribbing collar, keep it on the horse when he is in the pasture. The horse may choose cribbing over interaction with the other horses.

Horses can also use mounted feed buckets for cribbing. You can put your horse's feed bin on the ground, so he will not crib on it.

Cribbing is not to be confused with wood chewing. People often equate cribbing to wood chewing, but that is a mistake. Wood chewing does not involve sucking in air like cribbing does. The horse nibbles on the stall wood as if he is trying to eat it. Wood chewing is a bad habit just like cribbing. This is another cause of boredom. It causes damage to the horse's teeth and to the stall wood, and worse, splinters in the horse's gums or tongue.

Some people have a theory that wood chewing is caused by a vitamin or nutrient deficiency, however, no scientific research has yet proved this.

Wood chewing can be controlled by spraying the horse's stall with some foul-tasting substance. These products can be found at saddlery shops or you can find them online. Use only products that are specifically for stalls to stop wood chewing. These products are safe is the horse swallows it. Using your own method, such as tabasco sauce, can be harmful to horses.

Bad Stall Habits

Stall weaving is another common bad habit. Stall weaving is when the horse is standing at the stall door poking his head out (this is when the stall has a top door that opens so the horse can stick his head out). The horse makes a swaying motion back and forth, sometimes with the eyes half closed. The hind legs stay in place and the head and front legs move from side to side.

Stall weaving, like cribbing, may be caused by stress or boredom from excessive stall confinement. This may happen especially when your horse is kept in a stall and can see his friends running around and having fun in the field. Your horse does not understand why he cannot go out and play and gets anxious and stressed. Only you know why he cannot go out and play. This is like a child in school having to stay in during recess while the other children go outside and play (the difference is, the child knows why he/she must stay in).

It's a Jungle Out There!

Excessive stall confinement is the common cause of colic, which is the worse. Excessive stall confinement is also the cause of most known bad habits, also called vices. Another bad habit caused by excessive stall confinement is barn sourness. When a horse is barn sour, that means the horse does not want to leave the barn. He views the barn as his sanctuary and thinks his life will be in danger by leaving the barn. Barn sour horses are given ample amounts of food and water, but they are not put out in the pasture enough. When a barn sour horse is taken too far away from the barn, he will fight his handler and want to bolt back towards the barn. Correcting this takes work, time and patience. The obvious correction is to keep him out in the field, preferably with other horses, if this can be done, and ride him in areas away from the barn. Taking your horse on trail rides accompanied by familiar horses is a good way to get your horse to enjoy time away from home.

You will never correct barn sourness by letting the horse stay in his stall. In fact, you are just enabling it more. Keeping him in the stall and catering to his fears only worsens the issue. He will never conquer his fears if you give in to him rather than correct the issue.

When Dexter had a full day's work, such as when practicing for a horse show, he was ready to get back to his stall. But in that case, it was understandable. It could be like you being at the office for the whole day and you are ready to get home.

There's No Place Like Home

I have the "travel bug" and I am the type of person who wants to see the world. During my travels, I wanted to go and not come back (I had to return home, not because I wanted to).

We know not every person has the "travel bug." Neither does every horse. In fact, it is very rare to find a horse who enjoys traveling.

I took Dexter to many places away from home, and even to Canada for a show. Dexter traveled well although he was nervous the day of arrival. This is why for shows, we took the horses to the new place a day or two before the show.

Barn sourness can be compared to people who have not traveled enough during their lives. Some people are afraid to go more than 10 miles away from their homes. Those types of people can only handle a short time away from home before they get homesick. That is how a barn sour horse feels.

I started traveling when I was young. This got me wanting to get out more and explore new places. I did not let a "comfort zone" confine me to home.

The more you get out, the more you enjoy being outdoors and are not afraid of the world, along with exploring new places. The concept is the same for correcting a barn-sour horse.

Pawing

Pawing is another bad stall habit. The horse scratches the ground with his front hoof. This looks like a bull that is ready to charge, except the horse does not do this out of aggression. Pawing the ground is a sign of nervousness or anxiety. If the horse could talk, his words could be "I just want to get out of here!" or "are we done yet" or "when do I go back to my stall?"

It could be like a person fidgeting, such as when someone is anxious to get out of some place they do not like. This means the horse is getting impatient, such as he wants out of his stall, or wants to go back to the barn, or wants food. While riding, the horse may paw at the ground to get back to the barn. Excessive pawing can cause hoof damage and even laminitis.

Stall Kicking

Stall kicking is another bad habit. This can be caused by the horse wanting feeding or a treat, or he wants out of the stall to get away from his neighbor, or just wants to run around in the field. Stall kicking is another sign of anxiety or impatience. Stall kicking causes damage to the horse's hoof and leg, and to the stall walls. One way to solve this is to move the horse to a different area of the barn (if it is because of his neighbors) and line the stall walls with padding. Do not give the horse food or treats to stop stall kicking. This will just reinforce his bad behavior.

Stall kicking can also be caused by two horses who do not get along in neighboring stalls. Those horses want to get away from each other. When you were a child in school, did you ever sit next to someone you did not like, and ask to be moved away from that child? This is a similar concept with "enemy" horses next to each other.

It is often hard to tell which horse is more aggressive and causing the commotion. If you find which horse is the aggressor, move that horse to a stall on the end, preferably one not next to another horse, such as in a stall next to a tack room.

Just like with people, bad habits have to be corrected, not catered to. With horses, it takes work and patience to correct bad habits, but it can be done.

Chapter 7: Your Partnership with Your Horse

When Dexter was brought to the stable, I was determined to make him my partner. Therefore, I treated him good, and wanted to spoil him!

You want to enjoy riding your equine companion, whether he is new to you or you owned him for a while.

First, you want to be sure your horse's tack fits properly. Improperly fitting saddles can cause distress lead to bad habits. The same applies with the bridle. If the bridle does not fit or you use the wrong kind of bit, the horse will associate the saddle and bridle with pain and cause him to avoid being saddled up. The horse knows what the saddle and bridle are – and he will know the equipment will lead to.

Making the Ride Enjoyable for You and Your Horse

Horseback riding builds trust between the horse and rider. If a horse is not treated properly when ridden, he will not want anyone on his back. Therefore, you do not want to keep kicking him or beating him or pulling on the bit in his mouth. Otherwise the horse will dread having you on his back.

You want to avoid people who mistreat you, right? This is how the horse feels when he is around people who mistreated him.

Imagine you are giving someone a piggyback ride and they kept kicking and beating you. You would throw that person off your back immediately!

You want the horse to be your partner. You would not want him to think "I am not going to work with this crazy creature that walks on his hind legs!" Therefore, you have to treat him right when riding him.

Some horses can be "remote-control". Another term used is "mechanical". These horses are very obedient and will do what they are told, like a robot. They do not fight the rider. These horses are good for beginners, but experienced riders have been known to get spoiled by riding a "mechanical" horse. Although experienced riders find or more relaxing and taking a break from a horse that has a mind of its own, experienced riders should not get attached to "mechanical" horses. Besides, you want your horse to be your companion like a person, not like a robot.

Dexter was far from mechanical. He had a mind of his own indeed! However, riding a horse like Dexter was good training for me.

From the Horse's Mouth

For the bridle, be sure you use the proper type of bit. The bit is the metal bar that goes in the horse's mouth.

A bit too harsh, such as one that is for more active and energetic horses, can cause pain and will not correct the horse. The wrong type of bit will cause the horse to avoid being bridled. You would not want your horse to dread having the bridle put on.

Beginner and novice riders make the mistake of constantly pulling on the reins to avoid the horse going too fast. This causes pain to the horse and will make him bit-shy. You should imagine a metal bar in your mouth and someone constantly pulls on it. That would hurt. Horses have feelings too and they can feel pain. This is a cause of horses becoming hard to bridle.

The worse mistake riders make is jerking down on the horse's reins to correct his bad behavior. This is WRONG! First, it does not correct the horse's bad behavior. Second, it causes the horse excruciating pain in his mouth and jaw and can even lead to dental issues. This another cause (if not, the main cause) of horses become resistant to having the bridle put on. As stated before, horses are intelligent animals and know what to associate riding equipment with.

Dexter was hard with the bridle at first, because his former owners constantly jerked on the reins to correct bad behavior. When bridling, he would raise his head up all the way to avoid the bridle. I often had to call an instructor to help. I had to use a plain and simple bit and I had a good instructor who taught me to be easy on the bit in his mouth. Over time, Dexter became more manageable getting the bridle on.

Bitless bridles are becoming more common. I wish these were around during the days when I had Dexter.

Using a bitless bridle has resulted in more responsiveness from the horse as well as making him more comfortable. A bitless bridle puts pressure on the nose rather than on the mouth. Bitless brides have even been used in some high-level competitions in some regions. Horse show judges are becoming more horse-friendly and know a metal bar in the horse's mouth can be distracting.

Be sure your horse is comfortable wearing the tack. If he is not comfortable, you must find and correct the issue. Do not use a saddle that is too small which can cause sores. Also, be sure the girth is not too tight. The girth is the belt that goes around the horse's belly, which holds the saddle up. A tight girth interferes with the horse's breathing and can cause the horse to buck to get rid of the discomforting girth. That would be light you putting your belt on too tight. You have hands to remove the belt. The horse cannot remove the saddle girth.

Do not make your horse deal with the pain of bad-fitting tack. Constantly saying "stop it" will not stop anything. If he acts up due to bad-fitting tack, do not get aggressive with him. That would be like someone making you wear clothes or shoes that do not fit. You will not be comfortable and would get upset having to wear bad-fitting clothes or shoes. When something is not fitting right, they will let you know.

Do Not Fall for Myths

Dexter was, by all means, an intelligent horse. There were times I felt like, especially during shows or when out on the trails, he was smarter!

People who think horses are stupid animals may have watched too many movies or TV shows. Perhaps they read George Orwell's book "Animal Farm" or saw the movie. The horse in "Animal Farm" is Boxer. Boxer is a huge, strong draft horse (either a Clydesdale or Shire) but had low intelligence. In real life, draft horses are quite intelligent.

Horses are more intelligent than what they are given credit for. People who are not experienced with horses fall for the myth that horses are stupid animals. Believing this myth can put you in a precarious situation.

A horse can tell if his rider or experienced or not. If a beginner rides a horse with a mind of its own and just wants to fight the rider, the ride may not be fun. This also can discourage the rider from future horseback riding experiences. Horses can take advantage of beginner riders and the horse will become the boss. This causes the horse to think he can get away with anything, including gorging on grass while riding. The horse will know that a beginner rider does not know how to use the reins and is unable to pull the horse's head up while the horse is grazing.

Horses can also figure out how to open gates and stalls. This is not something you just see on movies- this is real life. That is why stall and gate latches must be horse-proof, so the horse cannot open them using his mouth.

Apart from riding, smart horses have been known to open their stalls then open the door to the grain room. This leads to serious danger. A horse can literally eat himself to death if he gets in the grain room.

Exercising Basics

Horses are athletic animals and need exercise. They need plenty of room to run around.

Exercise is essential for horses, just like how it is for humans. Exercise prevents obesity and digestive issues, and just like in humans, exercise is good for blood circulation.

I am the type of person who cannot sit in one place for too long (except when I am on a plane flying overseas). When I reach my destination, I want to get out there and explore, and walking is good exercise.

Water, please!

After workouts, horses need to drink water. If you have been around horses for a long time, you may have been told to never give a horse water right after a workout. Doing so could cause the horse to get very sick or even colic. This is a myth that has been debunked.

When I had Dexter, I was told not to let him drink after working out. Even back then, I thought that was cruel. What I would do is allow Dexter to take a few swallows from a bucket, walk him some more, then let him have a few more swallows. As he cooled down more, I let him have more water.

Imagine you run a track and field race and you were denied water. That is torture. You would be seriously dehydrated by the time you could drink water. The same is true for horses. Waiting until the horse has cooled down to give him water can be dangerous.

This myth came about because possibly the horse drank very cold water too fast while overheated. You may have seen the part in "Black Beauty" where the horse was put in his stall while overheated (right after a strenuous workout) and gulps down a whole bucket of ice-cold water. Black Beauty gets seriously ill, and it was believed that the ice-cold water was the culprit.

The part of the story that is true is a horse should never be put in his stall immediately after a strenuous workout. He should be slowly walked to get his heart rate back down to normal. However, he should be given water, and must drink it calmly. To avoid him drinking too much water at once too fast, do not fill the water bucket to the top. If he drinks from a full bucket, it will be hard to pull him away.

When a horse is severely dehydrated, he can show colic-like symptoms. To avoid a dehydrated horse gulping down water too fast, thus making the symptoms worse, give him a half a bucket of water to start with. Walk him around some more, then gradually increase the amount of water (as I explained with Dexter earlier in this chapter).

I Know Who You Are

Horses can also tell different people apart. They know who is who. They know whether this person treats him well when riding or who has been abusive. Always approach your horse in a friendly manner and he will be nice to you in return.

Horses know if their owners are known to overwork them and cruelly treat them. If your horse associates you with getting a heavy workout and being pushed to the limit, you will learn this when trying to catch him in the field. When he sees you walk towards him with that lead line in your hand, his reaction would be "uh-oh!"

He will try every trick in the book to avoid you. Do not let your relationship with your horse come to this. Correcting this will be a challenge and may result in you having to "bribe" him to bring him in from the field. Furthermore, he may have to be kept in his stall when you are coming out to ride him. This will upset him because he will not understand why he cannot go outside with the other horses.

You want your horse to view you as a friend, including when riding him. When riding your horse, you want him to be your teammate and not your slave.

You want your horse to be happy when he sees you. Greet him with kindness and give him a treat.

Overworking your horse can deteriorate your relationship with him. When your horse is exhausted, let him rest. Do not keep urging him to keep running when he is breathing heavily. Going for gallops may be fun for you, but too much will tire your horse out, and he will not find it fun.

Maintaining a Healthy Relationship with Your Horse

Getting along with your horse must start from day 1. If you find that you and your horse are not getting along, it is best to move on to another horse. A broken relationship with a horse is not as easy to mend as a relationship with another person.

Keep treating your horse as your friend. If properly trained and treated, he is willing to work for you. You should work for him in return. Let him associate you as his friend and caretaker and not a brutal master.

Unfortunately, a relationship with a horse sometimes deteriorates over time. Nobody can pinpoint the cause – it just becomes like something that ran its course. Sometimes people who have been friends for many, many years end up going their separate ways for unknown reasons.

This results in the horse being sold and the owner having to find a new horse. The results are stress on both the horse and the soon-to-be former owner.

You may have difficulty finding out what went wrong over time. Obviously, there is some underlying cause, as something caused either the horse or you to change. Sometimes people never find the answer. They just know it is not working out and must sell the horse. The owner finds out that keeping a horse wasn't meant to be and does not buy a new horse.

Chapter 8: If You Must Sell Your Horse

Saying Goodbye

Dexter had to be sold because I was starting high school at a private school, which was an increased expense for my family. As we know, owning a horse is not cheap. That was hard on me, but it had to be done.

Horses did not leave my life. I still rode on weekends, taking lessons on the school horses at the local stable.

When owning a horse, to me it was not worth the expense unless I could be out there every day, which was hard while going to school in another town.

This is not the route people want to take. Sometimes they do not have a choice, which was my case. If it comes to the time you must part with your horse, either because your relationship with him is broken or your financial situation changes, and you can no longer afford him, first do your due diligence and find a reputable buyer. When you first bought your horse, you had every intention to keep him happy and healthy, but sometimes things change, and not always for the better.

You do not want to accidently sell your horse to an abusive person or worse of all, to a meat buyer. You want your horse to be happy in his new home, most importantly you want to keep him alive and healthy.

While in the age of technology, we can find out information on a person and whether or not this person is a horse lover or abuser. Thanks to the internet, an individual's information is not as private as it used to be.

A Picture Paints a Thousand Words

When we sold Dexter, this was long before the days of the internet. We had the old-fashioned ad in the paper with a black-and-white picture.

We all know we live in the digital age. This includes the age of smartphones. You may be tempted to take a picture with your smartphone, but it may not produce as good quality pictures as a digital camera. Digital cameras as not becoming "extinct" due to smartphones any time soon. The resolution of a digital camera is significantly better than a smartphone.

We are in the age of the internet which is slowly replacing newspapers. You can Google search horses for sale and check prices for horses in your area. List your horse's price a bit higher than the others, and you can negotiate. Be sure your ad is descriptive and do not hide any flaws, etc. The age of the internet is useful for showing videos. You can post a video of someone riding the horse to give the buyer a better idea how well the horse behaves. Include videos of the basics, such as walking, trotting and cantering. If the horse is a jumper, include some jumping videos. Also include the number of, and pictures of prizes the horse has won in events. More descriptive history is more appealing to buyers.

When going the old-fashioned way of placing ads in the newspaper, be sure to have a good conversation with the potential buyer and ask for information if this person has previously owned a horse. You will want to know this person's history with horses.

Visitation Rights

You sold your horse and you miss him. Keep in contact with the new owner and ask if you can visit your former horse. Of course, it all depends on where the horse has moved to. A long-distance move may make this impossible. If your horse is sold to someone local, ask if you can visit your former horse. This will also assure you your former horse is doing well in his new home and has a loving and caring owner.

I visited Dexter a few times in his new home. From what his new owner said, he was happy in his new home. I was glad.

You may find out that the new owner treats him better and takes care of him better than you did. This is common. You may ask yourself what stopped you from treating him so well like that. Do not let it get you down. You should focus on your former horse being happy. If you are buying a new horse, you will learn from those mistakes. Hopefully, if you go the route of buying a new horse, you can have a loving relationship with your new horse.

Not Buying Another Horse? You have Options

After finishing high school and starting college, I knew buying another horse was out of the question. Even to this day, working a full-time job, there is no way I could afford a horse.

If you decide that it is too much work and trouble, both mentally and financially, the option of leasing may be better. The old-school term used is share boarding. With share boarding, you get access to the horse without the responsibilities such as feeding, vet costs, farrier costs, and so on. You share the expenses with the horse's owner. Some horse owners are away or are working full-time and need help maintaining the horse. Share-boarders are sort of like secondary owners. A share boarder will pay the owner a fee (either monthly or weekly) to keep the horse exercised and maintained. This helps the owner make money to put towards the horse. Share boarding is also a cheaper option if you ride frequently and do not want to pay each time you ride a stable's horse.

Keep in mind that a horse you share board is still owned by someone else. You are still in the "back seat." Therefore, the owner still has priority when it comes to riding the horse or showing him in events.

In addition, share boarding may not be worth the costs unless you can ride the horse often. Maybe not every day, but most owners want a share boarder to ride the horse at least two or three times a week.

Here is my current situation - if you cannot ride often, such as you work a full-time job and can only ride on weekends, then paying per ride may be a better option. You can ask the stable manager if you can ride a lesson horse for an hour or two, without taking a lesson. The term often used is called a "hack". Please do this only if the stable manager knows you well. Never ask if you and the stable manager recently met.

Keep in mind not all stables have this option – you may be required to take a lesson in order to ride. Lessons are good for any level. Never think you are too good to have a lesson.

I am now a retired show jumper, but I still ride for pleasure. I take lessons at my local stable (not jumping anymore). The instructor knows I am not training for shows anymore so our lessons are basic. That does not mean I am treated like a beginner. I still do the walk, trot and canter, but at my pace – not at the instructor's.

If you do not want to take a lesson and want to enjoy nature, check for trail riding in your area. I have some trail riding places in my area. Although I join beginners, I have no issues. When some in the group hear that a retired show jumper is joining them, they say that makes them feel safe.

Just because you end up becoming a horseless horse lover, do not give up hope. Owning a horse is not for every horse lover (with finances being the main obstacle). As described earlier, you do not have to get horses out of your life if you find you are no longer in a position to own a horse. A horseless horse lover still has opportunities!

About the Expert

Karin Bauer is a widow with no children. She is a freelance writer and blogger. She is also an entrepreneur. She runs three online business and enjoys sales and marketing.

Formerly a New Jersey state government employee, Karin left her job for new opportunities. She wanted to have more time for traveling and writing about her travel adventures.

Karin has been riding horses for over 30 years. She used to compete in show jumping events, but now rides for pleasure. She rides the horses at her local equestrian center and helps care for them.

Karin has traveled to many countries and includes horseback riding in her travel plans. She embarks on adventurous horseback riding vacations while traveling.

From the Expert

I hope you reading enjoyed reading this book and have learned about horses and how to care for them. From bringing a horse home to building the relationship, it can be a long and rewarding journey. The duties of maintaining a horse never stop, but I hope all the hard work and money put in becomes worth it to having a life-long friendship with your horse!

Keeping building a friendship with your horse, and you could enjoy him more than any human companion!

HowExpert publishes quick 'how to' guides on all topics from A to Z by everyday experts. Visit HowExpert.com to learn more.

Recommended Resources

- HowExpert.com – Quick 'How To' Guides on All Topics from A to Z by Everyday Experts.
- HowExpert.com/free – Free HowExpert Email Newsletter.
- HowExpert.com/books – HowExpert Books
- HowExpert.com/courses – HowExpert Courses
- HowExpert.com/clothing – HowExpert Clothing
- HowExpert.com/membership – HowExpert Membership Site
- HowExpert.com/affiliates – HowExpert Affiliate Program
- HowExpert.com/writers – Write About Your #1 Passion/Knowledge/Expertise & Become a HowExpert Author.
- HowExpert.com/resources – Additional HowExpert Recommended Resources
- YouTube.com/HowExpert – Subscribe to HowExpert YouTube.
- Instagram.com/HowExpert – Follow HowExpert on Instagram.
- Facebook.com/HowExpert – Follow HowExpert on Facebook.